CONTRIBUTORS

John E. Allen

Sue Becklake

Robert Burton

Barry Cox

Jacqueline Dineen

Plantagenet Somerset Fry

Bill Gunston

Robin Kerrod

Kaye Orten

Peter Stephens

Aubrey Tulley

Tom Williamson

Thomas Wright

ARTISTS

Barbara Bailey

John Barber

Richard Eastland

Gill Embleton

Vanessa Luff

Stephanie Manchip

Sean Rudman

George Thompson

Mike Whelply

Photo Credits
Heather Angel; Ardea;
Bruce Coleman; Jeff Goodman;
Alan Hutchison; A. G. Leutscher;
Natural History Photographic Agency;
S. Walker.
Front cover: Natural History Photographic
Agency

CHIEF EDUCATIONAL ADVISER

Lynda Snowdon
Infant School Headteacher

TEACHER ADVISORY PANEL

Helen Craddock
Infant School Headteacher
John Enticknap
Author and Primary School Headteacher
Arthur Razzell
Lecturer in Child Development,
Author and Headteacher

EDITORIAL BOARD

Philip M. Clark   Executive Editor
Rosemary Canter   Editor
Frances Middlestorb   Picture Researcher

DESIGNERS

Faulkner/Marks

ISBN 0 333 252799 (volume 9)
    0 333 194446 (complete set)

© Macmillan Publishers Limited, 1979

First Published in 1979 by
Macmillan Children's Books
a division of Macmillan Publishers Limited,
4 Little Essex Street, London WC2R 3LF
and Basingstoke

Associated companies in
New York, Toronto, Dublin,
Melbourne, Johannesburg and Delhi

Printed in Hong Kong

Cold-Blooded Animals

Contents

COLD-BLOODED ANIMALS

All animals are related to each other. They are divided into two groups. You can see the cold-blooded animals in the blue circles. Their bodies are at about the same temperature as their surroundings. The warm-blooded animals are in the pink circles. Their bodies have a high temperature which always stays the same.

frog

crocodile

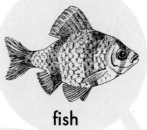
fish

starfish

shark

sea-urchin

tortoise

worm

jellyfish

sea
anemone

coral

snail

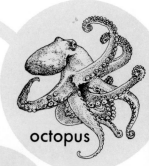
octopus

sponge

mussel

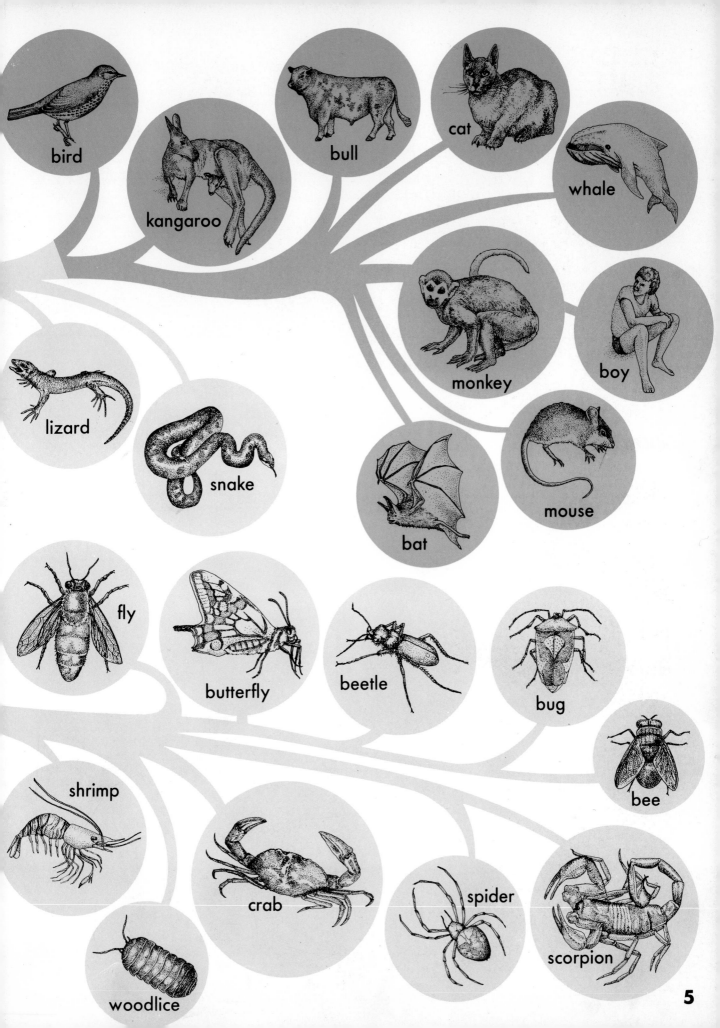

bird

kangaroo

bull

cat

whale

monkey

boy

lizard

snake

bat

mouse

fly

butterfly

beetle

bug

bee

shrimp

crab

spider

scorpion

woodlice

SIMPLE ANIMALS

Mammals, birds, reptiles, amphibians and fishes have skeletons of bone. Their skeletons have a backbone with rows of bones called vertebrae. These animals are called vertebrates. You can feel your vertebrae in the middle of your back. Animals that do not have backbones are called invertebrates.

The boy has a skeleton with a backbone. The worm he is holding is a simple animal. It does not have a skeleton and its body is floppy. The crab's body and legs are covered with a hard shell which is a kind of skeleton.

sea anemone

The sea anemone has a soft body.
Its tentacles sting fish and push food
into its mouth. When the tide goes
out the anemone closes up its
tentacles. This keeps it moist.

Sponges are animals, not plants.
The bath sponge that we use is the
skeleton of the animal. It is made up
of strong fibres. Sponges live mainly
in warm, shallow seas.

sponge

Animals of the garden

The garden is the home of many simple animals without backbones. You can find these animals on plants, in the earth or in ponds. Sometimes you have to look very carefully. Slugs and snails have soft bodies. They do not like hot, dry weather. When it is hot, snails hide in their shells. Slugs creep into the shade.

ladybird

wolf spider

greenflies

ants

beetle

slugs

earthwor

snail

earwig

8

Earthworms live underground but they come up to eat leaves at night. Moths also come out at night. You can see most of the animals in this picture in the daytime. Butterflies and bees fly from flower to flower. Ladybirds and spiders eat other animals. Ants eat a substance called honeydew.

white admiral

bumble bee

honey bees

large heath butterfly

peacock butterfly

wasps

garden snail

9

Animals of the rock pool

The seashore is a very good place to look for animals. When the tide goes out, sea creatures are left in rock pools. Can you see the prawns and blennies swimming in this pool? Sea anemones, mussels and barnacles are fixed to the rocks, but limpets and topshells can crawl around slowly.

The giant clam lives on coral reefs. It grows up to one metre across and weighs up to 250 kilograms.

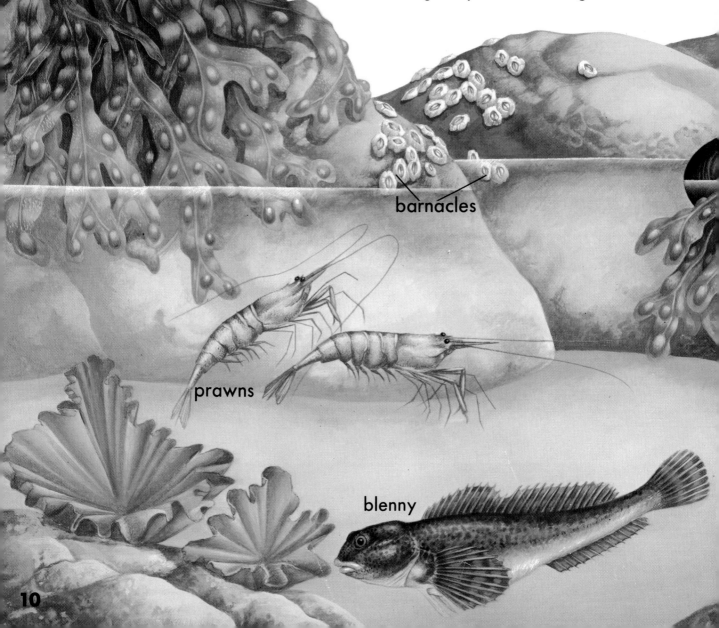

barnacles

prawns

blenny

Starfish live in the sea, but they
sometimes come into rock pools.
They eat mussels and other shellfish.

limpets

barnacles

mussels

sea anemones

blenny

topshells

Octopuses and squids

All molluscs have soft bodies. Molluscs such as winkles, clams and limpets are protected by hard shells and move slowly. Octopuses and squids are molluscs which do not have a shell. They live in the sea and can move very fast. Their long arms have rows of suckers. They use these suckers to catch their food.

octopus

An octopus has eight arms. It walks on the sea bed or swims by squirting a jet of water. It kills its prey with a poisonous bite.

A squid has ten arms. It also moves by squirting out a jet of water which pushes it forwards. Giant squids grow up to 20 metres in length. This giant squid is having a long battle with a sperm whale.

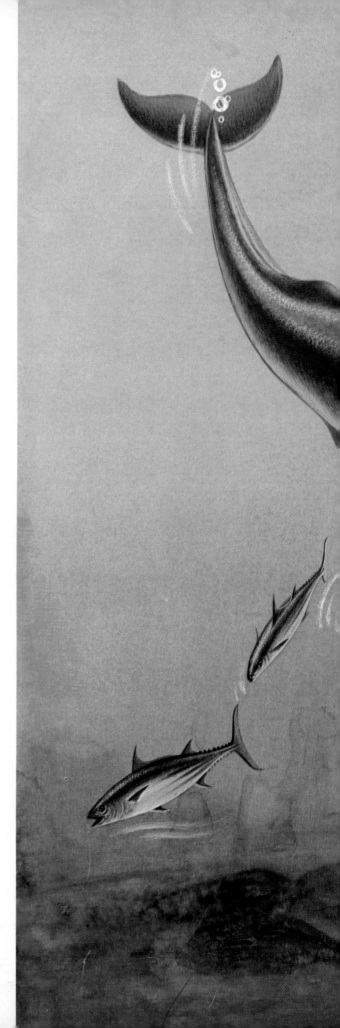

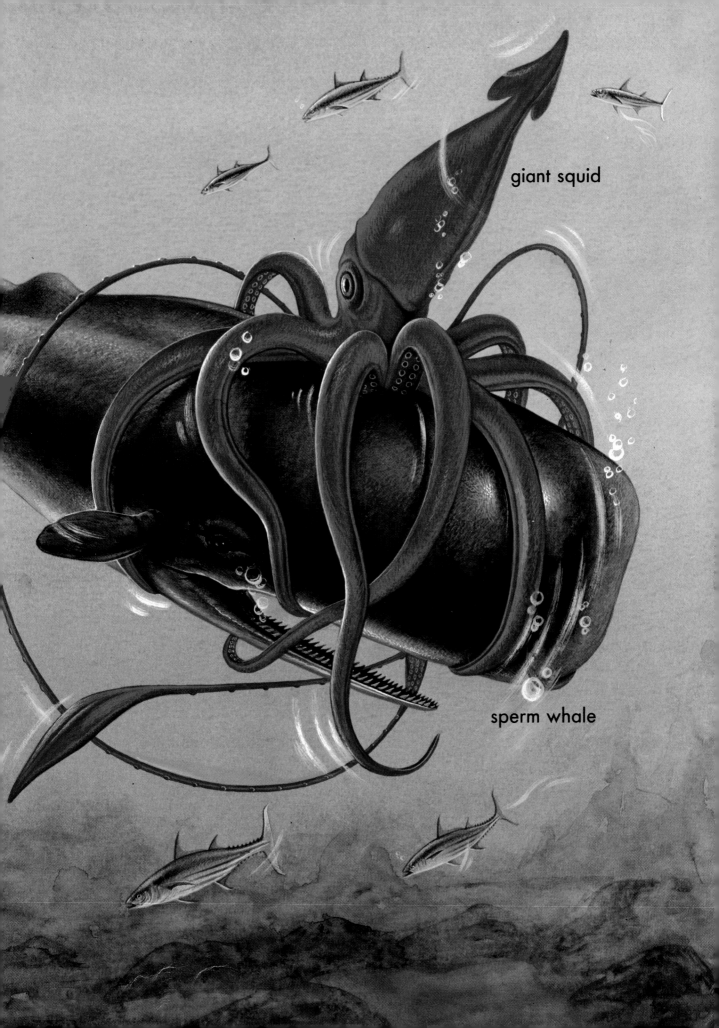

giant squid

sperm whale

ANIMALS WITH MANY LEGS

Most animals with backbones have four legs or fins. Some stand upright on their back legs. Others use their tail as a kind of third leg. Animals without backbones have all sorts of arrangements of legs. Some of them have very strange ways of walking. Some animals, like the worm, have no legs at all.

0 legs

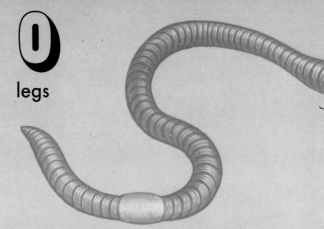

A worm has no legs. It moves by pushing out its head and then pulling the rest of its body forwards.

1 leg

A snail crawls on its stomach which is a kind of foot. It lays a sticky trail to help it slide along.

2 legs

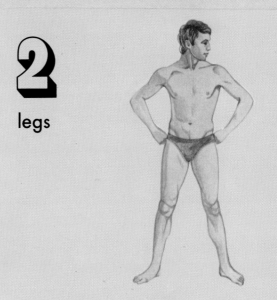

A man stands upright on his two legs.

3 two legs and a tail

Kangaroos use their tail for balance.

4 legs

Bears usually walk on all fours.

14

5

four
legs
and a tail

This monkey uses its tail as a fifth leg to help when it is climbing through the trees.

6

legs

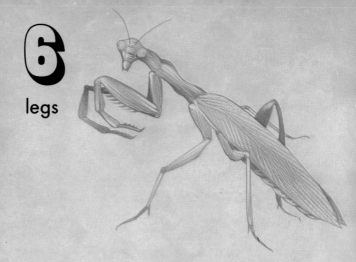

The six-legged mantis is an insect. It catches food with its front legs.

8

legs

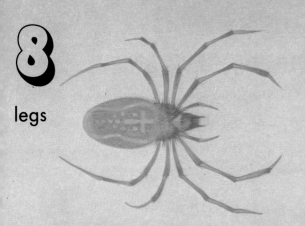

Spiders have eight legs. The extra pair of legs makes them different from insects.

10

legs

Crabs have ten legs. The front pair are claws which are used for fighting.

30+

legs

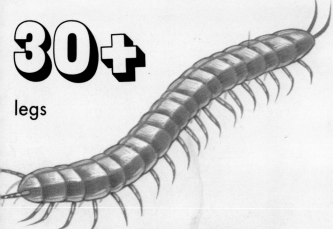

A centipede has one pair of legs under each section of its body.

60+

legs

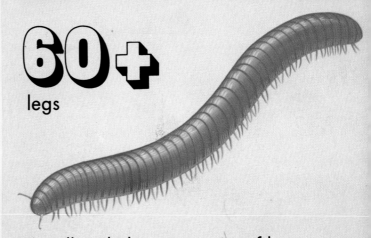

A millipede has two pairs of legs under each section of its body.

Crabs and lobsters

Crabs and lobsters are called crustaceans. Their bodies are covered with hard skin. This skin is their shell. When they are growing, they shed their skin and grow a new one. They have five pairs of legs, but the front pair are large claws which they use for fighting and for catching food. Most crabs and lobsters live in the sea.

The shore crab is very common in rock pools and on the beach. It eats any animals that it can seize with its claws. It also uses its claws to defend itself. If you try to pick up a shore crab, it may nip you with its claws.

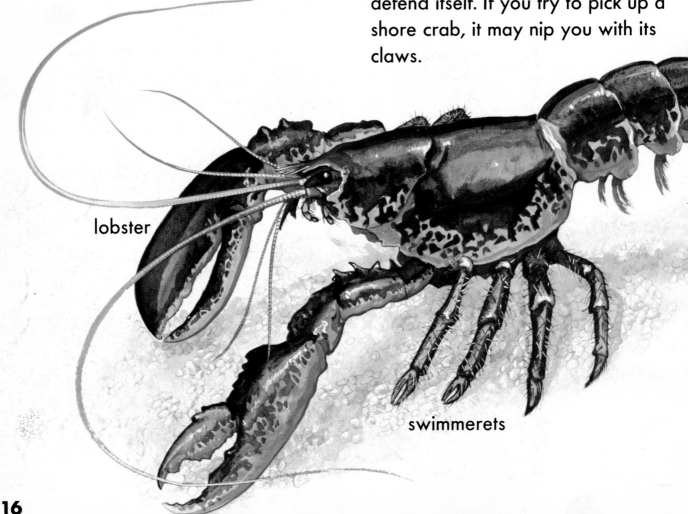

lobster

swimmerets

Fiddler crabs have one huge claw. They use it for signalling to other crabs. Fiddler crabs are found round the coast of Britain.

Lobsters have very long bodies and several pairs of legs which they use for swimming. These legs are called swimmerets. Fishermen catch lobsters in lobster pots like the one on the right. The lobster climbs into the pot to get food but cannot get out again.

Shrimps and barnacles

Shrimps and barnacles are both crustaceans but they look very different. A shrimp looks like a tiny lobster and can swim very well. A barnacle looks like a limpet. It has a hard shell. When a barnacle is covered with water its shell opens. The barnacle then waves its legs around to catch food.

Baby barnacles float in the sea. When they are older they fix themselves to something solid. They usually fix themselves to rocks. Sometimes they stick to the sides and bottoms of ships. In the picture above you can see men scraping barnacles off the side of a ship.

This shrimp is living in a razor-shell, where it is safe from its enemies. It only comes out to feed.

When the tide goes out barnacles shut their shells and are safe until the tide comes in again. Shrimps are often trapped in rock pools. They are easy to catch.

Spiders and scorpions

All insects have six legs. Spiders and scorpions have eight legs so they are not insects. Scorpions have a front pair of claws like a lobster. They have long bodies and their tail has a sting in the tip. Spiders have round bodies.

scorpion

Scorpions use their claws for catching food. They only use their sting to defend themselves.

This spider has caught a fly in its web, and has wrapped it in silk before eating it.

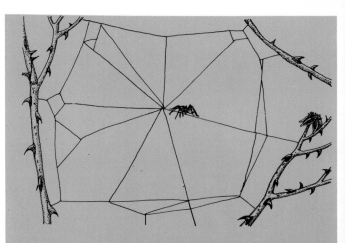

To build a web the spider first makes a frame of silk threads.

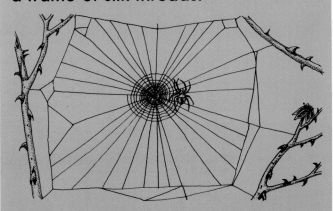

Next the spider lays a spiral of silk thread on the frame.

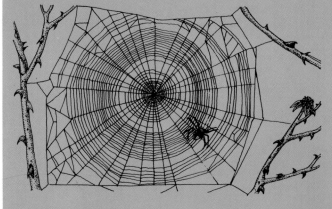

When the spider has finished making the web, it sits and waits for flies to be trapped in it.

This spider is waiting patiently in its web. When a fly is caught by the sticky silk it struggles. This struggling warns the spider. The spider runs across the web and kills the fly by poisoning it.

INSECTS

You can recognize an insect because it has three pairs of legs and its body has three parts. Most insects lay eggs but some give birth to baby insects. Some young insects look like their parents. They are called nymphs. Others have soft, worm-like bodies. These are called caterpillars or grubs. They change into adults inside a case. This case is called a pupa.

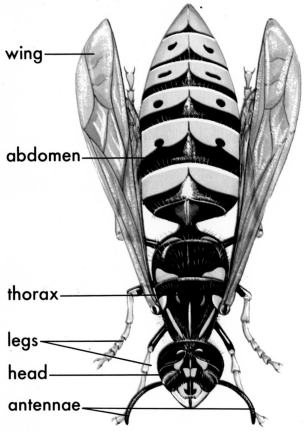

wing

abdomen

thorax

legs

head

antennae

The body of an insect, like this wasp, has a head, a thorax and an abdomen. The wings and legs are joined to the thorax.

The life of a butterfly or moth starts with an egg. You can often find insect eggs on leaves.

The pupa splits open and the adult butterfly or moth crawls out. Adults do not usually live very long.

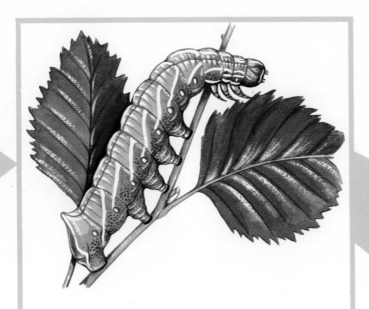

The egg hatches into a caterpillar.
The caterpillar spends most of its
time eating. It grows very fast.

chrysalis

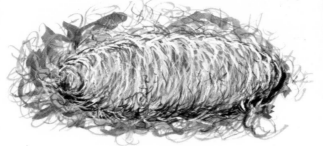

silk cocoon

The caterpillar turns into a pupa.
A butterfly pupa is called a chrysalis.
Moths spin a silk cocoon.

Butterflies and moths

The wings of butterflies and moths are covered with tiny scales. They are often very brightly coloured. The best way to tell a butterfly from a moth is to look at its antennae. A butterfly's antennae end in knobs. A moth usually has feathery antennae. Most butterflies feed on nectar, from flowers.

garden tiger moth

Most moths fly at night and hide by day. The garden tiger moth cannot hide very well. It is too brightly coloured. The elephant hawk moth only comes out on warm summer nights. Its caterpillars have a coat of long hair.

elephant hawk moth

The bull's eye moth in the picture above and the emperor moth have 'eyes' on their wings. These 'eyes' scare away birds that may try to eat the moths. Most moths have wings that fasten together with a tiny hook. Butterflies do not have these hooks.

emperor moth

monarch
butterfly

swallowtail
butterfly

common blue
butterfly

peacock
butterfly

Butterflies do not look as if they are strong fliers but some kinds travel long distances. The monarch butterfly of America flies 3000 kilometres to spend the winter in warm countries. Sometimes it flies across the Atlantic Ocean. Swallowtails and blue butterflies usually stay in one place.

Brazilian skipper butterfly

Many insects die at the end of the summer. Peacock butterflies, like the one on the left, are different. They live in hollow trees and in buildings during the winter. In the spring they wake up and fly away. You can see them in many different places. They make their homes in parks, gardens and forests.

Flies

Most insects have two pairs of wings. Flies have only one pair. Instead of the rear pair of wings they have two tiny stalks. These stalks help the fly to keep its balance when it is flying. Some flies are very dangerous because they carry disease. Mosquitoes carry a disease called malaria which can kill people.

You must never let house-flies walk on food in the kitchen or in the shops. These pictures tell you why.

Flies carry germs on their feet. Germs cause disease. When you eat the food, you also eat the germs.

Daddy-long-legs is another name for the crane-fly. It has long, thin legs which break off easily. The grubs of crane-flies are called leather-jackets. They live underground.

The germs soon make you ill. So always cover food. It is best to keep food in a refrigerator.

Hover-flies look like wasps but they
cannot sting you. They can hover
and fly backwards just like a
helicopter.

House-flies have feet which have two
claws and a rough pad. These help
the fly to walk on walls and ceilings.

Pond animals

There are some kinds of insects which live in ponds. Dragonflies fly over ponds and lay their eggs in the water. The water beetle and the water-boatman live in the pond. All these insects eat other animals. You can see a baby dragonfly called a dragonfly larva in this picture. It eats the larva of other pond animals.

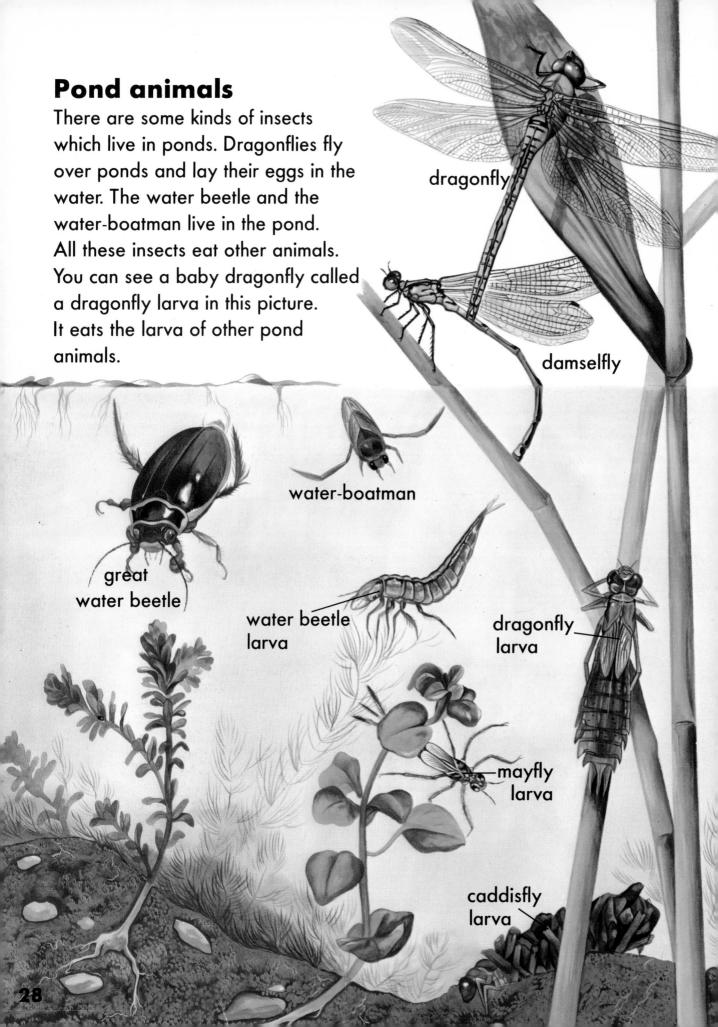

dragonfly

damselfly

water-boatman

great
water beetle

water beetle
larva

dragonfly
larva

mayfly
larva

caddisfly
larva

Termites

Termites live in huge nests, like the one on the right. These nests are like castles made of hard earth. Often the nests are as much as five metres in height. Termites live in warm countries like Australia and parts of North and South America. Their main food is wood. They often attack wooden buildings.

A termite nest is the home of a queen termite and thousands of worker termites. There is also a king termite. The enormous queen termite grows up to five centimetres long. She does nothing but lay eggs.

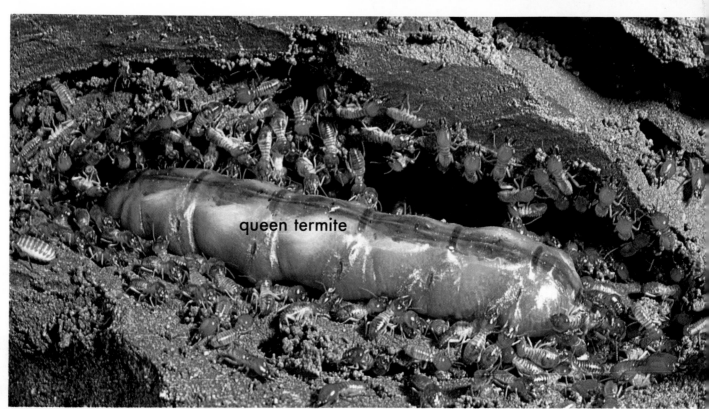

queen termite

Grasshoppers, crickets and locusts

Grasshoppers and crickets have long back legs. They can jump well. If you try to catch one it will leap away. They also have wings for flying. Grasshoppers and crickets usually come out in warm weather. You can see grasshoppers in the daytime but crickets mostly come out at night. Locusts are a kind of grasshopper.

The skins of insects cannot stretch. As insects grow they shed their old skins and grow new ones which are larger. This grasshopper is climbing out of its old skin.

Locusts live in hot countries. Sometimes they gather in great swarms. These swarms are called 'plagues of locusts'. Young locusts are called hoppers. They cannot fly. Swarms of winged adults and hoppers can destroy fields of crops.

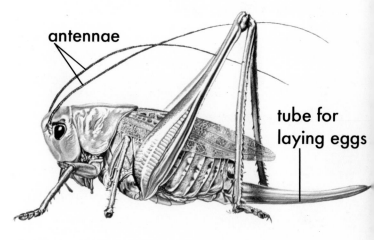

Crickets have longer antennae than grasshoppers. This female cricket has a long tube at the end of her body. She pushes this tube into the ground and lays her eggs through it.

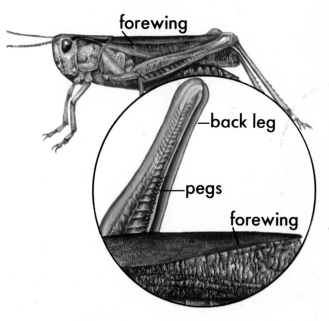

A grasshopper's back leg has a row of pegs along one side. It 'sings' by rubbing its back leg against its forewing. The picture in the circle above is a close-up of the grasshopper's leg and forewing.

Beetles and bugs

Beetles have hard, shiny front wings which are often brightly coloured. These front wings protect the delicate back wings.

A bug is an insect. Its mouth has a hollow tube rather like the syringe a doctor uses for injections. The tube has a sharp tip and is used for sucking up food.

greenflies

stag beetles

Greenflies are bugs which suck the sap from plants. Gardeners get rid of greenflies and other bugs because of the damage they cause.

These beetles are called stag beetles because their large jaws look like the antlers of a stag, or male deer. You can see these male stag beetles using their jaws for fighting.

This ladybird is taking off from a plant. You can see its brightly coloured front wings.

Ladybirds are beetles. They eat greenflies and other bugs.

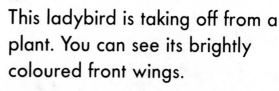
backswimmer

The backswimmer or water-boatman always swims on its back. It rows along with its back legs. It is a bug which sucks the blood of other animals. If you touch a backswimmer it may sting your finger.

Bees wasps and ants

Bees, wasps and ants live in large nests. In each nest there is a female, called a queen, who lays eggs. The eggs hatch into grubs. The queen is helped by the worker insects who look after the nest and collect food. In summer, young queens mate with males and fly away to start new nests.

The young queen bee is accompanied by a crowd of worker bees, called a swarm.

A worker wasp eats ripe fruit. It also catches insects for the young grubs.

swarm

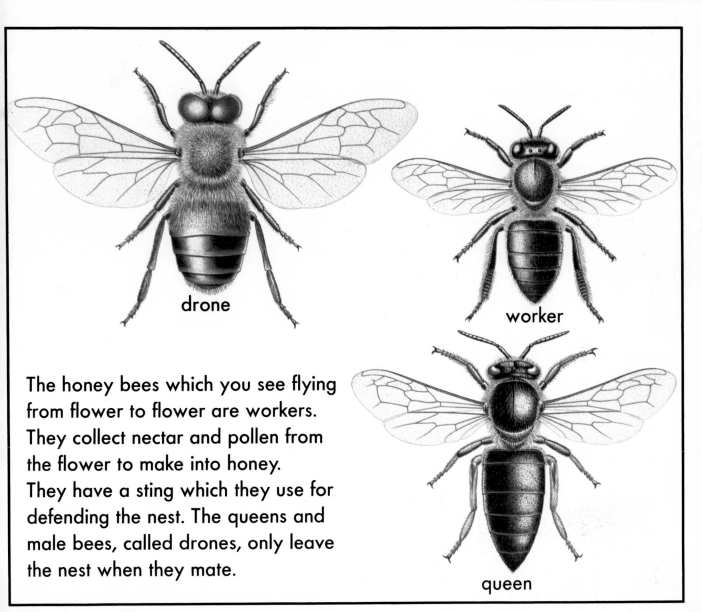

drone

worker

queen

The honey bees which you see flying from flower to flower are workers. They collect nectar and pollen from the flower to make into honey. They have a sting which they use for defending the nest. The queens and male bees, called drones, only leave the nest when they mate.

Worker ants do not have wings like bees and wasps. They have to walk when they are searching for food. They are very small, but they are strong. They can easily carry food many metres back to the nest.
The parasol ant on the left is carrying a flower to its nest. Parasol ants eat a fungus that grows on the flower.

FISH

Fish are the oldest animals with backbones that we can find today. Nearly all fish live in water. Lungfish and some other fish can come out on land for a short time. Fish swim by wriggling their tails. Their fins help them to keep their balance and steer. Their bodies are covered with scales.

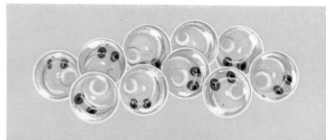

Most fish lay eggs. A few give birth to baby fish. Some fish look after their eggs until they hatch.

water in

gills

water out

A fish needs oxygen to breathe. It gets its oxygen from water. The fish takes in a mouthful of water. Its gills take oxygen from the water and then squirt the water out again.

You can keep fish in a tank of water called an aquarium. Rocks and weeds make the aquarium look like a pond.

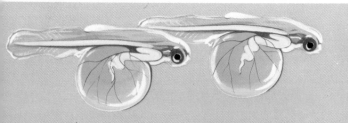 

The egg hatches into a larva. At first the larva carries a bag of yolk which it feeds on.

The yolk slowly disappears as the fish grows up. The fully grown fish in this picture has fins and a tail.

fish in aquarium

Sharks

Sharks are fish whose skeletons are made of soft cartilage instead of bone. Most sharks have very sharp teeth and eat fish. Great white sharks are fierce hunters. They sometimes eat men. Blue sharks and leopard sharks can also attack people.

blue shark

thresher shark

great white shark

leopard shark

hammer-head shark

Sharks are a danger to divers, who often carry weapons to defend themselves. Sharks do not always attack, as the picture above shows.

Some sharks give birth to live young. Others lay eggs in cases. These cases are called 'mermaids' purses'.

Sea fish

The coral reefs of tropical seas are
the homes of many amazing fish.
There are strange seahorses and
brightly coloured clownfish and
butterfly fish. Some of the fish that
live in coral reefs are dangerous.
The lionfish has a nasty sting.
The moray eel lives in crevices.
It has sharp teeth and sometimes
bites divers.

seahorse

scorpion fish

clownfish

puffer fish

angel fish

butterfly
fish

bat
fish

sea anemone

moray eel

River fish

These are fish which live in lakes and rivers. Some of them are good to eat. The brown trout lives in clear streams. It eats insects which land on the surface of the water. When it has grown up, the eel swims down the river to the sea. The pike is a fierce hunter which eats other fish. Small fish are eaten by kingfishers as well.

kingfisher

pike

barbel

dace

brown trout

dace

chub

eel

tench

Unusual fish

There are thousands of different kinds of fish. Many of them look very strange. Some have very odd habits. There are fish which live on the bottom of the oceans and have rows of glowing spots on their bodies. There are fish that can glide through the air. There are even fish that can climb trees.

Surgeon fish, like this one on the right, live among coral reefs. They have bones near their tails that are as sharp as a surgeon's knife.

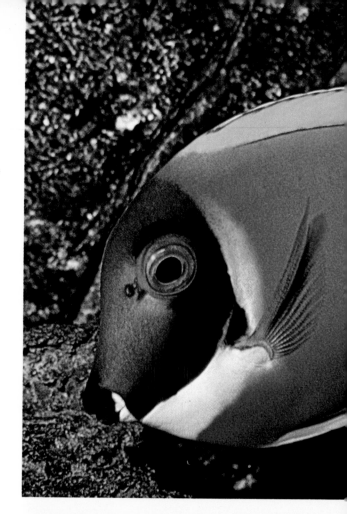

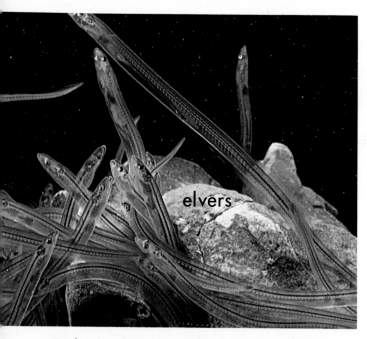

elvers

Baby eels are called elvers. Elvers swim thousands of kilometres from the warm sea where they hatch to the rivers of North America and Europe.

seahorse

The seahorse is one of the oddest fish. It swims by moving the fin on its back. The female lays her eggs in a pouch on the male's belly.
The babies swim out after hatching.

On the left is a puffer fish. This fish can blow up its body like a balloon. This makes it difficult for enemies to swallow.

Amphibians

Amphibians are animals which can live either on land or in the water. Their eggs do not have shells and have to be laid in water. The adults' skin is not fully waterproof and it has to keep moist. A few amphibians do, however, live in dry places.

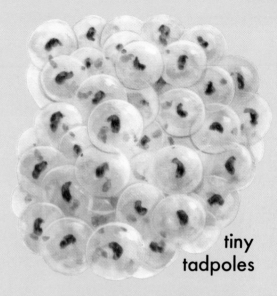

tiny tadpoles

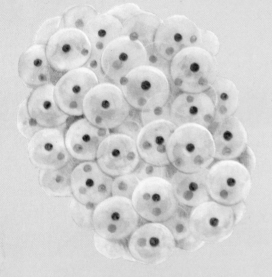

Frogs' eggs are covered with jelly. The jelly protects the eggs from enemies and keeps them warm.

You can see the eggs developing into tiny tadpoles. It takes about two weeks from laying to hatching.

At first, the tadpole has no legs. It looks rather like a fish and breathes with gills.

two days old

six days old

In the picture above you can see the tadpole six days after hatching.

On the left you can see clumps of frogspawn in a pond. The parent frog leaves the spawn as soon as it is laid.

As the tadpole grows bigger, it starts to grow legs. The back legs appear first. The front legs are hidden by the gill flaps.

six weeks old

eight weeks old

After twelve weeks, the tadpole begins to look like a frog. The tail starts to shrink.

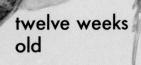

twelve weeks old

The adult frog has no tail and hops on its legs. It breathes with lungs.

Most amphibians lay eggs which hatch into tadpoles. The tadpoles may look very different from their parents. They live in water and gradually change into adults. Then they leave the water and live on land. When they have grown up, they return to water to lay their eggs, called spawn.

adult frog

Frogs and toads

Frogs and toads are amphibians without tails. The largest is the goliath frog of Africa. It is 30 centimetres long. Frogs and toads walk or hop on land. In the water they swim with a breast stroke, like a human swimmer. Frogs have smoother skins than toads and longer legs.

Frogs and toads sing with croaks and grunts. This reed frog blows up its throat like a balloon when it sings.

The male midwife toad carries spawn from the female on his legs. He has to keep the spawn moist.

Tree frogs live in hot countries.
They can climb well and jump from
branch to branch. Their bright green
colour matches their surroundings.

Newts and salamanders

Frogs and toads are amphibians without tails. Newts and salamanders are amphibians too, but they keep their tails when they are grown up. They look like lizards, but they have damp skins. When they run, they wiggle their bodies from side to side. Like other amphibians, they eat small animals.

Fire salamanders, like the one you can see below, live in Europe. People used to think that fire salamanders could walk through fire without being burned. This is not true.

The giant salamander comes from North America. It climbs trees and barks when alarmed.

The axolotl which you can see in the picture on the right is a salamander which never grows up. It spends its whole life as a tadpole.

When the time comes to lay eggs, newts gather in ponds. The male newts, like the one below, become brightly coloured.

Australian
rock
python

The Australian rock python curls
around her eggs to protect them
from enemies. She stays with them
until they hatch.

REPTILES

Reptiles are animals which can spend all their lives on land. Their skins are covered with scales and are waterproof. Reptile eggs have a leathery skin and are laid on land. The eggs of some reptiles hatch inside the mother's body and the baby reptiles are born alive.

Millions of years ago the dinosaurs and other giant reptiles were the most important land animals.

The tuatara, which you can see in the picture above, is a very ancient reptile. It looks rather like a lizard. It lives on islands near New Zealand.

Reptiles are cold-blooded animals. Lizards warm their bodies by basking in the sun, like the one on the left. They can run faster when they are warm. At night lizards hide in holes or under stones to keep warm.

lizard

Lizards

Lizards are reptiles which usually have slender bodies and tails. The shingle-back lizard is fatter than other lizards. The frilled dragon runs on its back legs. The goanna has strong, curved claws but the gecko has special soles on its feet so that it can cling to walls. The legless lizard crawls like a snake.

legless lizard

shingle-back lizard

leaf-tailed gecko

spotted goanna

frilled dragon

Crocodiles

Crocodiles live near water and they can swim well. Some kinds of crocodiles live in the sea. Crocodiles usually eat fish but they can kill large animals by drowning them. They can grow up to eight metres in length. Crocodiles are now becoming very rare. Alligators and gharials are two kinds of crocodile.

American alligator

gharial

Siamese crocodile

Tortoises and turtles

Tortoises and turtles are reptiles with hard shells. Some kinds can pull their head and legs into the shell for safety. Tortoises live on land. Turtles live in water. Turtles' legs have developed into flippers which they use for swimming. They lay their eggs on land.

This giant tortoise is big enough to carry a boy on its back. Some giant tortoises live for over 150 years.

The green turtle lives in the sea. It eats a kind of grass which grows on the sea bed. Turtles come ashore to lay their eggs in the sand.

tu

tortoises

Tortoises grow very slowly and live for a very long time. They cannot walk very fast. They protect themselves by pulling their head and legs into their shell. Tortoises usually eat plants but they sometimes like to eat slugs and worms. Pet tortoises can be very big or very small.

terrapin

Terrapins are small turtles. They live in freshwater ponds and rivers. Red-eared terrapins, like the one above, are often kept as pets.

Snakes

Snakes are reptiles without legs. They eat other animals and can open their mouths very wide to swallow large animals. Some snakes are poisonous. Others kill their victims by squeezing them to death.

Snakes are deaf and cannot hear the snake charmer's music. They sway in time to the man's movements.

This game of snakes and ladders shows some colourful snakes.

California king snake

adder

scarlet snake

cobra

gaboon
viper

green mamba

garter snake

rattlesnake

ATTACK AND DEFENCE

Cold-blooded animals have many different ways of harming their enemies. Bees and wasps sting to defend themselves. Poisonous snakes bite when they cannot escape. Other animals attack when they are looking for a meal. Some animals spread diseases when they suck blood.

Jellyfish can sting small animals which they then eat.

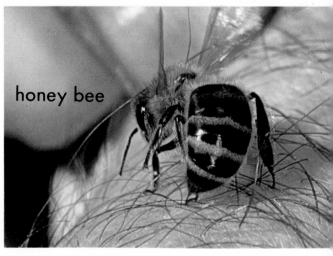

honey bee

The honey bee stings by injecting poison through a tube at the tip of its body.

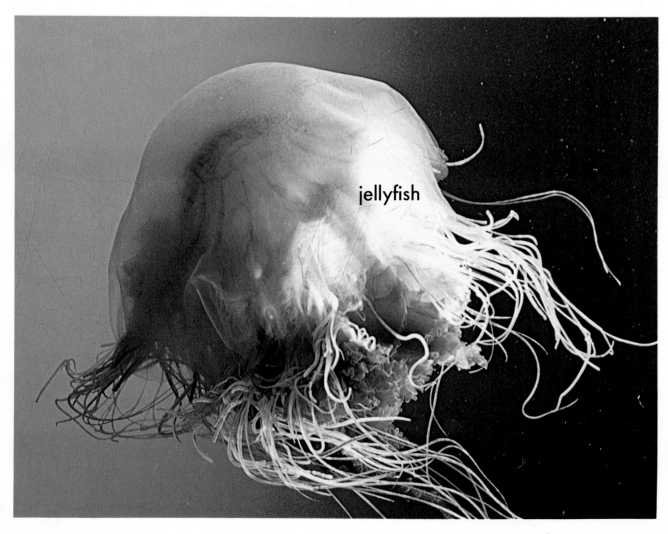

jellyfish

leech

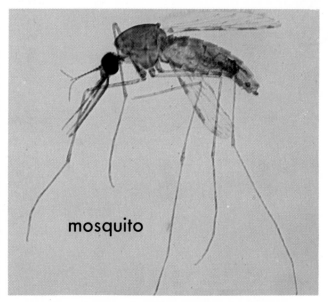

mosquito

Leeches, like the one in the picture above, cling to the skin of an animal and suck its blood.

piranha

Mosquitoes suck blood through a hollow tube. In hot countries they spread malaria and other diseases.

Piranhas are small fish. They attack large animals which wade or swim in the river.

Camouflage

Camouflage is a way of making things difficult to see. Animals are often camouflaged so that they cannot be seen by their enemies, or so that they can get near to their prey. The colours of the animals on this page match their background. The stick insect's shape also makes it difficult to see.

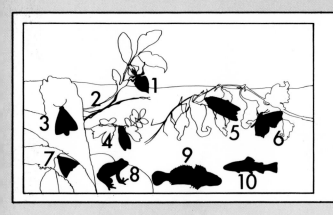

1 leaf insect   6 peacock butterfly
2 stick insect   7 carpet moth
3 goat moth   8 golden bell frog
4 cossid moth   9 bullhead fish
5 owlet moth   10 brown trout

DID YOU KNOW?

Many people keep cats and dogs as pets. These animals keep away rats and mice. In Borneo, some Chinese people keep pythons in their houses to scare away mice.

Sometimes snails go to sleep for three or four years. Once, a hungry snail woke up inside a letter box. He began to eat a letter. Somebody got a letter that the snail had nibbled!

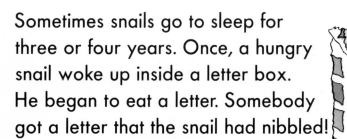

One Friday, two snakes in the London Zoo were fighting over their dinner. Then one snake swallowed the other by mistake. Now the keepers watch very carefully to make sure it does not happen again. Keepers in zoos look after their animals very well. There is a story that they once fitted a snake with a glass eye!

Tortoises eat leaves. Some leaves are poisonous, but the tortoises cannot taste the poisons very easily. This tortoise can taste poisons!

INDEX